TopGear
50
FASTEST CARS

STIG TESTED

BBC Children's Books
Published by the Penguin Group
Penguin Books Ltd, 80 Strand, London, WC2R ORL, England
Penguin Group (Australia) Ltd, 250 Camberwell Road, Camberwell,
Victoria 3124, Australia (a division of Pearson Australia Group Pty Ltd)
Canada, India, New Zealand, South Africa

Published by BBC Children's Books, 2012
Text and design © Children's Character Books, 2012

10 9 8 7 6 5 4 3 2 1

Written by Matt Master
Designed by Dan Newman, Perfect Bound Ltd
Content previously published in 100 Fastest Cars

ISBN: 9781405909020
Printed in China

TopGear
50
FASTEST CARS

Contents

Introduction

In the name of research, *Top Gear* has spent thousands of hours going fast on the *Top Gear* test track. After countless years, miles and miles per gallon, this is the ultimate list: *Top Gear's* fifty fastest cars.

Some of them you'll know very well, some you may never have heard of, some are brand new, some so old even your dad won't remember them. But trust us, this is the list to end all lists...

...because it's not about 0-60mph. And it's not even about top speed. It's not even about how fast it'll spin you round our track. It's more about that thing you can't really explain that makes your eyes pop and your hands shake. These are the fifty coolest cars that have ever went fast. These things are the reason that *Top Gear* set up in the morning, and the reason it can't get to sleep at night...

Cool Rating

It goes without saying that no car in this book is actually uncool (by which we mean a bit warm and clammy). But this **Stiggometer** should help separate the merely chilly without doubt from the seriously sub-zero... with love.

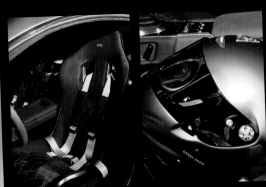

Aston Martin
DBS

If there is one person in the world that every car maker wants the official seal of approval from, it's got to be James Bond. Happily for Aston Martin he seems to like the DBS these days, just so long as it's fitted with a few hidden extras.

Aston's 510bhp V12 super-coupe is the ultimate blend of luxury and sporting ability, being both stupendously fast and posher inside than a private jet.

Although no match for its rivals from Ferrari and Lamborghini for pure pace, it exists in an entirely cooler world full of glamorous parties, beautiful style and deadly secret agents. OK, maybe not the secret agents, but you get the idea.

Power: 510bhp

0-60mph: 4.3 seconds

Top Speed: 191mph

Price: £170,500

Cool rating:

01

02

AC Cobra

1964

In the sixties a tiny British sports car company called AC was busy making a pretty little two-seater called the Ace. It was the sort of thing you took your girlfriend out in, maybe for a picnic in the countryside.

Meanwhile, in the USA, a burly chap in a cowboy hat called Caroll Shelby was tuning up enormous V8 engines and wondering what to do with them. You can guess what happened next.

The AC Cobra rocked the racing world and went on to become one of the most iconic road cars of all time. Simple, beautiful and with a turn of speed more commonly seen in surface-to-air missiles, there are few cars that capture the vision of a sports car more perfectly.

 **Power:** 260bhp

0-60mph: 5.5 seconds

Top Speed: 138mph

Price: £2500 (1967)

Cool rating:

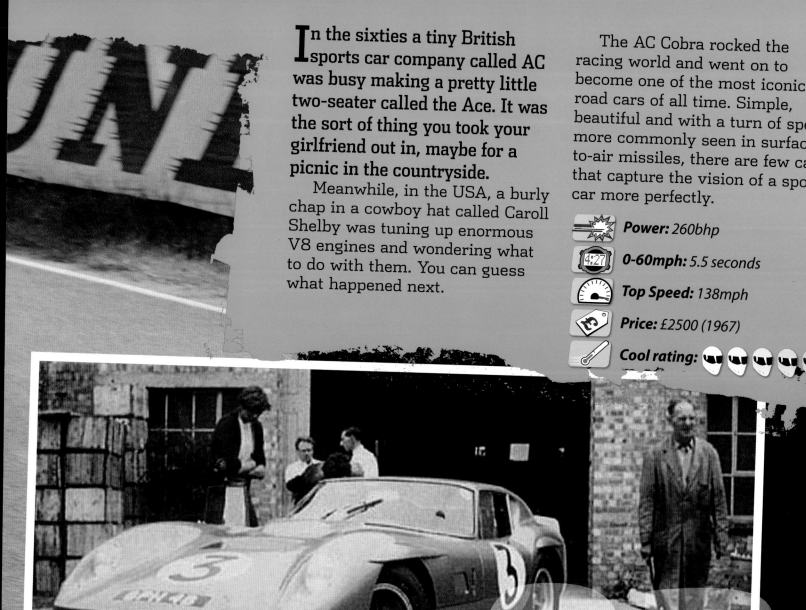

Vauxhall VXR8
Bathurst

DE51 RED

'I just **love** the sound of a supercharger!'

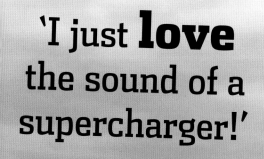

Ignore the Vauxhall badge. This is really a Holden, the Australian alternative to Vauxhall. What that means is that instead of a boring man with a briefcase and sandals, you get a hairy bloke in a sweaty vest.

The VXR8 is a car so macho that it makes rugby players hide behind their mums' skirts. It has a huge supercharged V8 taken straight out of the latest Corvette and creates enough noise when you stamp on the fast pedal to make animals drop dead in sub-Saharan Africa. When you're in Leeds. It's not very good to drive, but that's hardly the point is it?

 Power: 564bhp

 0-60mph: 4.6 seconds

 Top Speed: 155mph

 Price: £45,000

 Cool rating:

Even very sensible people like the men who work at Volkswagen have days when things go a bit loopy. Bored of putting 105bhp 1.6-litre engines into Golfs, a few mechanics decided to pinch a 6.0-litre 12-cylinder engine from the Phaeton limousine, bolt on two turbochargers and then see if they could squeeze it into a GTI.

Needless to say it didn't fit under the bonnet so they put it where the back seats were meant to be.

VW says that the 641bhp Golf W12 is capable of hitting 202mph. But it also says there are no plans to make more and sell them to the likes of us. (See. Back to being sensible again.)

 Power: *641bhp*

 0-60mph: *3.7 seconds*

 Top Speed: *202mph*

 Price: *Not for sale*

 Cool rating:

'It is an **insane** car, this.'

WOB·PS 650

GTI

04

Not everyone realises that Lamborghini started out making tractors. But anyone who ever bought a Countach worked it out pretty fast. Despite looking like it could go to the moon and back before most normal cars had even started, Lamborghini's eighties icon was a bit of a pig to drive.

It was enormous for a start, which never helps, and you needed legs like Mr Universe to operate the pedals. You couldn't see out of the back at all either, which made reverse parking an act of blind faith. Often a very expensive act at that.

But point a Countach down a windy mountain road and all was forgiven. This was a car that was made for that one thing, and is hopeless at everything else.

 Power: *375bhp*

 0-60mph: *6.8 seconds*

 Top Speed: *196 mph*

 Price: *£17,000 (1974)*

 Cool rating: 🏎🏎🏎🏎

05 Lamborghini
Countach

Gumpert
Apollo

'Ye gods! This is just something else.'

By the skin of its (probably very sharp) teeth, the Gumpert is the fastest car round the *Top Gear* track. Less than a second separates the top five, but this ugly-as-sin supercar has it by a whisker.

Really just a racing car with boring bits like lights and indicators stuck on afterwards, the Apollo can hit 225mph, but will cost you £275,000 for the privilege.

Gumpert claims that, thanks to clever aerodynamics and general scary speediness, you could drive the Apollo upside down on the roof of a tunnel. Surprisingly they haven't found anyone willing to give it a go yet though.

 Power: *789bhp*

 0-60mph: *3.2 seconds*

 Top Speed: *225mph*

 Price: *£275,000*

 Cool rating:

The new Audi TT is a good car, but not exactly the sort of thing blokes brag about to their mates on the footy pitch. It's always been a bit too girly for that.

Well, not any more. The RS badge that Audi only ever sticks on the fastest and scariest cars to leave the factory has finally made its way on to the TT's backside.

Remember that this is meant to be a small car, powered by weedy engines and bought by people who worry about their hairstyle. Now it's a small car that's been lifting weights. Fat tyres, a rear spoiler, four-wheel drive and 335bhp. Time to start bragging.

Power: *335bhp*

0-60mph: *4.7 seconds*

Top Speed: *155mph*

Price: *£45,000*

Cool rating: 😎😎😎

07

07

Audi TT

RS

Renault Clio
Williams

In the nineties, Williams was the team to beat in Formula 1 and the engines it used were made by Renault. This sort of partnership is very good for business, so the bosses at Renault decided to sign off a sporty version of the first Clio with Williams badges all over it.

The truth was that Williams had absolutely nothing to do with the car, but that didn't matter a jot to Renault. Or the people that bought them, as it turned out. Sticking a powerful two-litre engine into a tiny French hatchback and making it wider, lower and meaner-looking, created a car that people still beg, borrow and steal to get hold of today.

 Power: 145bhp

 0-60mph: 7.8 seconds

 Top Speed: 134mph

 Price: £13,000

 Cool rating: 👓👓

08

Ford Escort Cosworth

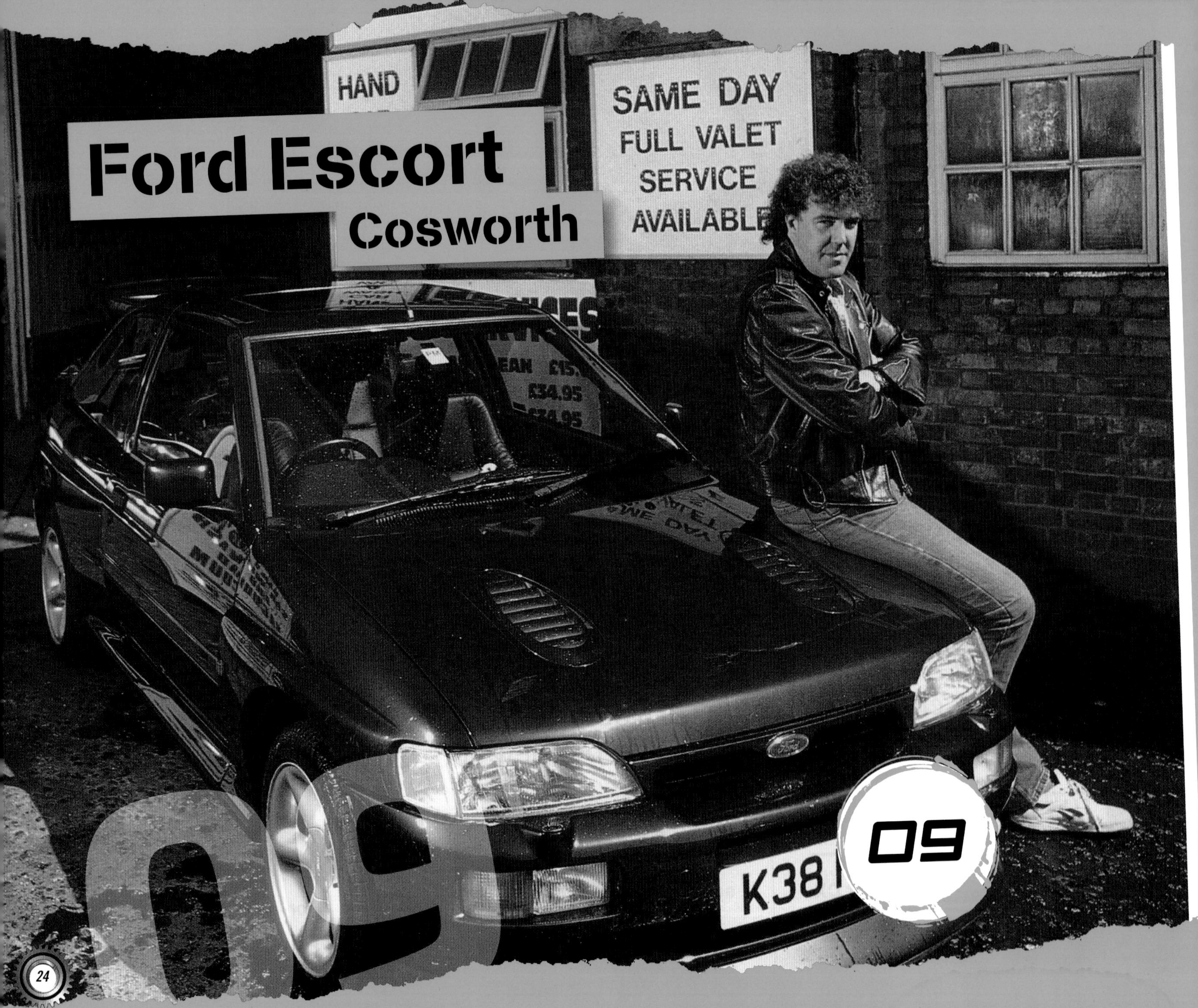

HAND

SAME DAY
FULL VALET
SERVICE
AVAILABLE

K38

09

When the Escort Cosworth went on sale in the early nineties it was an instant hit with a certain type of British bloke. And that type included one Jeremy Clarkson. Here was a bit of honest, local metal that looked like a cross between a proper racing car and a bouncer.

It had four-wheel drive, a huge twin-fin rear wing and a turbocharged Cosworth engine that people could, and regularly did, tune up to dizzying levels of power.

The only real drawback was that everybody wanted one and it was easy to steal. So that tended to happen rather a lot.

 Power: 224bhp

 0-60mph: 6.3 seconds

 Top Speed: 138mph

 Price: £26,000

 Cool rating:

Lotus rewrote the rules when it launched the first Elise way back in 1996. Here was a car that offered its driver almost nothing that you'd expect from normal 20th century transport. It was cramped, uncomfortable, had pretty much zero storage space, no back seats and even the stereo was an optional extra.

But it was more fun than a lifetime ticket to Alton Towers, and occasionally just as likely to make you feel sick.

So if you were willing to put up with a little discomfort, for the same money as a boring old hatchback, you could buy one of the best-handling cars of all time. And a lot of people did.

 Power: 118bhp

 0-60mph: 5.5 seconds

 Top Speed: 124mph

 Price: £19,000

Cool rating: 😎😎😎

10

10

Lotus Elise
S1

Ferrari 250
GTO

It may be one of the oldest cars in this book, but the Ferrari 250 GTO is also one of the greatest. Built to go racing in the early sixties, the GTO was an instant success on the track and just as quickly became immensely desirable in road-going trim.

With its blend of staggering performance for the time and the sort of looks that made men faint just as quickly as their girlfriends it soon became one of the most sought-after Ferraris of all time.

So much so, in fact, that in 2008 a GTO is rumoured to have sold for £15.7 million. You could probably buy the moon for that.

 Power: *300bhp*

 0-60mph: *6.1 seconds*

 Top Speed: *173mph*

Price: *£6000 (1962)*

Cool rating:

11

Mercedes CLK
GTR

12

The best way to make people think your cars are good is to win races in them. And if this isn't possible, maybe because your cars are a bit rubbish, then the next best thing is to make an unbelievably high-tech, lightweight race-rocket, and dress it up as one of your cars.

Mercedes aren't the only ones to have done this, but what they claimed was a CLK coupé under all the carbon fibre, wings and spoilers of their 215mph V12 racer was probably the furthest ever from road-going reality.

When it went on sale the GTR was also the most expensive production car in the world, costing over £1 million. And had a tendency to set itself on fire. These two facts don't sit all that well together, do they?

Power: *720bhp*

0-60mph: *3.4 seconds*

Top Speed: *215mph*

Price: *£1.1 million (1998)*

Cool rating: 🏎️🏎️🏎️🏎️

Porsche 911

GT1

13

There used to be a strange rule in sports car racing that said you had to sell a certain number of street-legal versions of whichever model you wanted to race. This was annoying for car companies but brilliant for us, because it meant Porsche had to make things like the GT1.

Although designed specifically to win the Le Mans 24 Hours, 25 GT1s were turned into road cars and sold to a lucky (and very wealthy) few.

Loosely based on the 911 of the time, the GT1 managed to squeeze around 700bhp from that car's 3.2-litre 6-cylinder engine and is rumoured to have been able to reach 235mph. Corking.

Power: 700bhp

0-60mph: 3.3 seconds

Top Speed: 235mph

Price: £550,000

Cool rating:

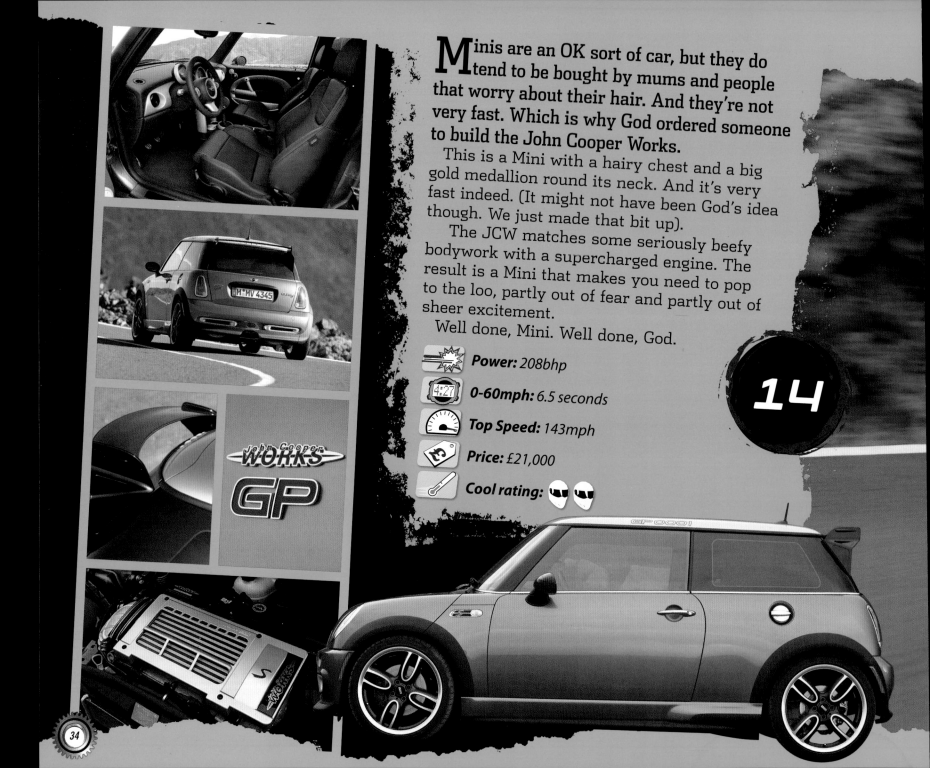

Minis are an OK sort of car, but they do tend to be bought by mums and people that worry about their hair. And they're not very fast. Which is why God ordered someone to build the John Cooper Works.

This is a Mini with a hairy chest and a big gold medallion round its neck. And it's very fast indeed. (It might not have been God's idea though. We just made that bit up).

The JCW matches some seriously beefy bodywork with a supercharged engine. The result is a Mini that makes you need to pop to the loo, partly out of fear and partly out of sheer excitement.

Well done, Mini. Well done, God.

Power: 208bhp

0-60mph: 6.5 seconds

Top Speed: 143mph

Price: £21,000

Cool rating:

14

MINI Cooper JCW

15

'It sounds like a Norse god of **thunder!**'

Koenigsegg
CCX

Sweden is a sensible country. Everything is very clean and tidy. Everyone is very polite. And Sweden makes Volvos, which are the world's most sensible cars. (And probably the dullest. Shhh.)

But tucked away in a quiet corner of the Swedish countryside is a place that makes the Koenigsegg CCX, the only car that has ever made the Stig need to call his mum.

This 806bhp monster is capable of reaching 245mph, making it one of the fastest road cars on planet Earth. And one of the scariest. After the Stig crashed one in 2008, *Top Gear* had to put a spoiler on it. Just to make his mum leave us alone.

Power: 806bhp

0-60mph: 3.2 seconds

Top Speed: 245mph

Price: £405,000

Cool rating:

Koenigsegg CCX

(with the *Top Gear* spoiler)

Chevrolet Camaro

Like its arch rival the Ford Mustang, the new Camaro is the reincarnation of a classic sixties muscle car. This means that it looks sort of old, sort of new, and like it's spent the last year locked in a gym.

Slotting the same V8 that powers the Corvette beneath its beefy body, the Camaro is that typical American mix of simplicity and power, with 426bhp fed to the rear wheels via a traditional manual gearbox.

In the USA a Camaro is cheap too, which makes you forget how rubbishy and plastic it feels, but evil things like tax make it very expensive in the UK. Expensive and still rubbishy and plastic? That's not so good.

 Power: 426bhp

 0-60mph: 4.7 seconds

 Top Speed: 155mph

 Price: £21,000

 Cool rating:

Although people are calling it 'The Baby Rolls', the Ghost is still more expensive than most peoples' houses, and about the same size.

Based on the not-very-babyish BMW 7-Series, and housing a not-even-remotely babyish 6.6-litre V12 under its enormous bonnet, the Ghost is still posh enough for the Prime Minister (probably far too posh actually), but as fast as most sports cars half its size.

It's almost 18 feet long and weighs more than Wales, but it can get to 60mph in well under five seconds and has been limited to 155mph. Just in case.

 Power: 563bhp

 0-60mph: 4.7 seconds

 Top Speed: 155mph

 Price: £195,000

 Cool rating: 😎😎

17

Rolls-Royce
GHOST

17

However big the engine, however sleek the bodywork, it's almost impossible to design a supercar that can outpace an Evo.

Using a really basic four-door saloon, but then sticking in all sorts of ingenious technology developed for racing rally cars, Mitsubishi can turn a shopping cart into a go-kart, producing something capable of giving a £200,000 Lamborghini Murcielago a run for its money. And for a quarter of the price.

The FQ400 gets 403bhp from a 2.0-litre, 4-cylinder engine while the Lambo has 631bhp from an engine three times the size. Makes you want to pay more attention in science class. Almost.

 Power: *403bhp*

 0-60mph: *3.8 seconds*

 Top Speed: *155mph*

 Price: *£50,000*

 Cool rating:

18

Mitsubishi Evo X
FQ400

18

'It is genuinely **incredible.** There is no car that handles like this one.'

43

While most really fast cars these days have their engines behind the driver and tend to look like ballistic missiles with wheels, Mercedes is doing it all very differently.

The SLS is a seriously modern supercar, but they've styled it on one of their most elegant sports cars from the sixties, the 300SL Gullwing.

This means the engine is out in front under a long menacing bonnet, and best of all, it also means you get those unbelievably cool gullwing doors. Definitely the car to have if you need to get places in a hurry but want to turn up looking sub-zero.

Power: 563bhp

0-60mph: 3.8 seconds

Top Speed: 197mph

Price: £130,000

Cool rating:

Mercedes SLS

19

45

'It looks good, it **sounds good** and it even puts a smile on your face every time the back end sets off on its own.'

MG SV

20

In the olden days MG was a brand for men with beards. And it still is come to think of it. But a few years ago, just before the company disappeared for good, it was about to launch a radical new sports car that would have blown the polyester socks off the old MG brigade.

The SV was a serious proposition, made entirely of carbon fibre to save weight and powered by a ferocious American V8 that could be tuned to up to 1,000bhp.

Or at least that's what MG said. Unfortunately we never got to find out because the money ran out before they could finish building the thing.

 Power: 320bhp

 0-60mph: 5.3 seconds

 Top Speed: 165mph

 Price: £75,000

 Cool rating:

A few years ago it was accepted everywhere in the world that Honda only made cars for Grandma. The only people that weren't happy about this were Honda. So they decided to build the NSX, a supercar to thrash Ferrari.

There was a lot of chuckling and raising of eyebrows, and then the NSX actually turned up. And it was amazing. It looked the business, went like stink and, best of all, was still as reliable and easy to use as Grandma's Honda Civic.

The last few ever made got the Type R treatment, which meant they were lighter, had racing suspension and were only ever painted white. A *Top Gear* hero.

 Power: 276bhp

 0-60mph: 4.4 seconds

 Top Speed: 168mph

 Price: £70,000 (–ish)

 Cool rating:

21

Porsche Cayenne
GTS

The Cayenne is one of those terrible cars favoured by footballers' wives and people with huge sunglasses and fake tans. Oh, that's footballers' wives again. Anyway, it's pretty awful. Not a proper Porsche, more of a posh handbag with four-wheel drive.

But the GTS is a bit different. Only a bit, mind, because it's still a terrible show-off, but at least this one drives like a Porsche should. It's quick, has a superb manual gearbox and handles better than any other SUV on sale today.

If you simply *have* to have a Cayenne (and you really don't, y'know?) then this is the only acceptable choice.

Power: *399bhp*

0-60mph: *6.1 seconds*

Top Speed: *157mph*

Price: *£54,500*

Cool rating:

Ferrari
458 Italia

23

Every time Ferrari launches a new car the world is left dumbstruck. Can it really look like that? Can it really go that fast? And the answer is always 'Yes'.

The 458 is Ferrari's latest mid-engine sports car, the model that will have every premiership footballer on the phone to his local dealer, begging and pleading and generally making a fool of himself.

It's worth the embarrassment though. The 458 is that perfect blend of stunning looks and astonishing performance. The V8 engine behind the driver pumps out 562bhp via a flappy paddle gearbox that borrows technology from Ferrari's latest Formula 1 car.

And one of the brains behind the 458 is none other than Michael Schumacher, just in case you were still having any doubts.

 Power: 562bhp

 0-60mph: 3.4 seconds

 Top Speed: 202mph

 Price: £160,000

 Cool rating:

'The acceleration is so **brutal!**'

Pagani Zonda F
Roadster

24

This is the car that even our very own Captain Slow fell in love with. Probably because the Zonda is everything a supercar needs to be: stunningly beautiful, absolutely unaffordable and insanely (by which we mean put it in a padded cell) fast.

With a 7.3-litre V12 engine borrowed from Mercedes, squeezed into a car that weighs as much as not very many tins of baked beans, the Zonda F Roadster will go from 0-120mph in less than 10 seconds and then get back to nought again in half that. It will, however, cost you £825,000 to try this, or it would if you could still buy a Zonda F. Which you can't. Sorry.

 Power: 641bhp

 0-60mph: 3.6seconds

 Top Speed: 214mph

 **Price:** £825,000

 Cool rating:

This is one of those cars that comes about because someone got really bored at work and their boss was off sick. When else does it seem like a good idea to stick a 3.0-litre V6 engine in the back of a Renault Clio?

The Renaultsport Clio V6 looks meaner than a pitbull in a biker jacket, but that's pretty much where the good news ends. Yes, it's very fast in a straight line, but keeping it in a straight line is almost impossible. There's also no room in there because the engine's in the wrong place. And to make matters worse, Renault had to make the V6 stupendously expensive to buy and *still* lost money on every one they ever made.

 Power: *255bhp*

 0-60mph: *5.8 seconds*

 Top Speed: *153mph*

 Price: *£27,000*

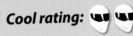 **Cool rating:**

25

Renaultsport
Clio V6

5945 WWT 92

There was a time when Aston Martin only made cars for really posh old men instead of footballers and people who've won the lottery. And back then the big, boxy V8 Vantage was Aston's sportiest model.

It had similar technology to a steam train and was even worse at going round corners.

But it was a lot better at going in a straight line.

This is what fans of ancient and rather rubbishy British engineering call 'point and squirt', meaning you point your car up the road, stamp on the gas and hope there isn't much call for turning the wheel.

It's a lot of fun and more than a little bit scary.

 Power: 438bhp

 0-60mph: 5.4 seconds

 Top Speed: 168mph

 Price: £20,000 (1977)

 Cool rating:

Aston Martin
V8 Vantage (Original)

 26

27

B MW don't muck about when it comes to building a fast car. But there is a company that still thinks they have a thing or two to learn.

Alpina is a little German outfit that has been giving BMWs a boost for over fifty years, so they definitely know their stuff. Sadly, when they got hold of the Z8, they turned it into the sort of car your granddad would use to find nice picnic spots.

Jeremy described driving the normal Z8 round a corner as 'like trying to get a wardrobe up a fire escape', and Alpina made it even more soggy and hopeless. Fast, and very beautiful, but a terrible way to spend £95,000.

 Power: *375bhp*

 0-60mph: *5.0 seconds*

 Top Speed: *161mph*

 Price: *£95,000*

 Cool rating:

BMW Z8
Alpina

Roush Mustang

When Ford brought out the new Mustang we all got quite excited. Until we found out it was rubbish. Another cheap, badly made American car that didn't go round corners and couldn't even go very fast in a straight line.

Then along came Roush, who got slightly bonkers racing experts fitted a supercharger to the Mustang, taking the power up to a whopping 430bhp. And that was the easy bit. Then they

set about making the Mustang handle properly, and did a pretty amazing job of that too. But the most interesting thing about the Roush Mustang is that it's still as cheap as Ford, Fiat and Volkswagen. If only we all lived in Texas.

Power: 430bhp

0-60mph: 4.9 seconds

Top Speed: 164mph

Price: £34,000

Cool rating:

28

This is the car that car nerds like us lot at *Top Gear* almost always call 'the most beautiful car in the history of the world ever'. Or something like that. The Miura really put Lamborghini on the map back in the 1960s and even now it is one of the most sought-after supercars for mega-rich collectors and film stars.

Truth be told, it was never actually very good. The designers put the fuel tank in the front and the engine in the middle, so that as you used up the petrol, the Miura began to do an involuntary wheelie. Not ideal at speeds of over 150mph. But no one cared then and no one cares now. Just look at it!

 Power: *350bhp*

 0-60mph: *6.2 seconds*

 Top Speed: *172mph*

 Price: *£6500 (1966)*

 Cool rating:

29

Lamborghini
Miura

This is one of those cars that, like Marmite, you either love or hate. The Alfa Romeo SZ can make girls swoon, but at the same time it'll probably make a few babies cry. In fact it was nicknamed *Il Mostro*, which is Italian for The Monster, and that was by the people who liked it.

But the SZ wasn't just about those weird looks. Brilliant engineering and the adventurous use of lightweight plastics meant that it was actually a fantastic car to drive.

Alfa made so few SZs that they are a very rare sight these days. But maybe you think that's a good thing...

 Power: 210bhp

 0-60mph: 6.9 seconds

 Top Speed: 153mph

 Price: £40,000 (1989)

 Cool rating:

30

Alfa Romeo SZ

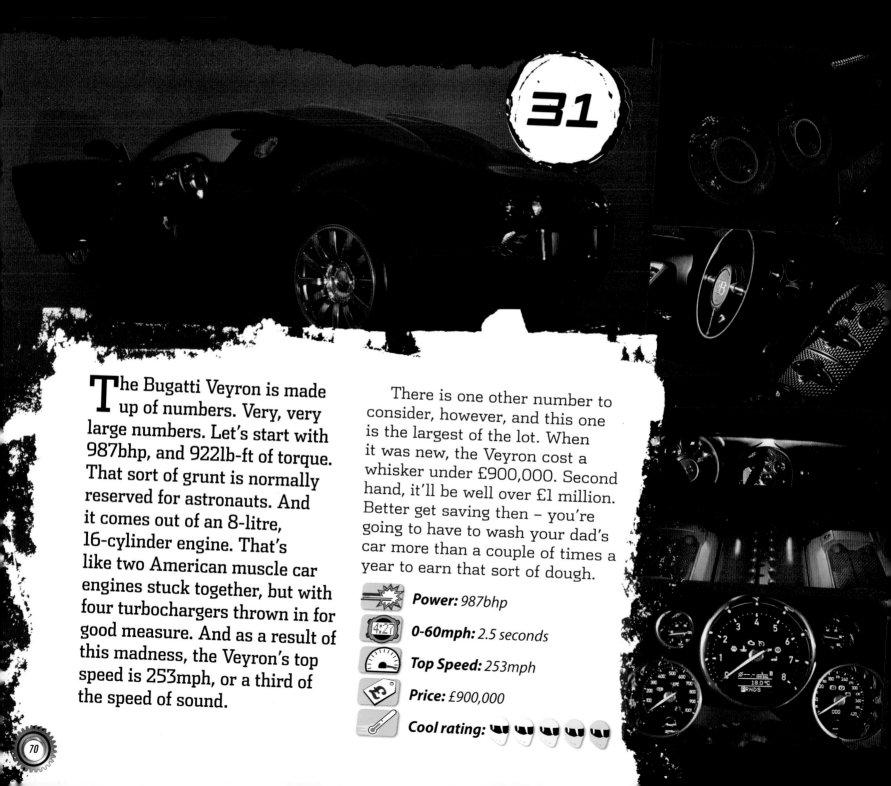

The Bugatti Veyron is made up of numbers. Very, very large numbers. Let's start with 987bhp, and 922lb-ft of torque. That sort of grunt is normally reserved for astronauts. And it comes out of an 8-litre, 16-cylinder engine. That's like two American muscle car engines stuck together, but with four turbochargers thrown in for good measure. And as a result of this madness, the Veyron's top speed is 253mph, or a third of the speed of sound.

There is one other number to consider, however, and this one is the largest of the lot. When it was new, the Veyron cost a whisker under £900,000. Second hand, it'll be well over £1 million. Better get saving then – you're going to have to wash your dad's car more than a couple of times a year to earn that sort of dough.

Power: *987bhp*

0-60mph: *2.5 seconds*

Top Speed: *253mph*

Price: *£900,000*

Cool rating:

31

Bugatti
Veyron

71

'That is proper head-alteringly **quick.**'

Noble M600

M600 GB

We Brits have a long and slightly iffy history of building plastic sports cars in leaky barns that are meant to be better than the latest Ferrari. Very occasionally they are, but mostly they don't even start.

Noble has made a fair few cars that are more familiar to the AA than their owners, but hopefully the brand new M600 will change all that.

With a twin-turbo V8 generating 650bhp nestled into a lightweight carbon fibre body, it's going to be faster than almost anything else on the road. And at £200,000 there won't be much that's more expensive. Fingers crossed it works...

 Power: 650bhp

 0-60mph: 3.0 seconds

 Top Speed: 225mph

 Price: £200,000

 Cool rating:

The logic behind the Viper is very simple. Big things have big engines. So why not take the 8.4-litre 10-cylinder engine and gearbox from an enormous truck and stick it in a sports car?

Turns out there are a lot of reasons why not. Driving the SRT-10 is still like driving a truck, just an unbelievably fast one that appears to have been made out of recycled crisp packets.

The Viper looks tremendous and sounds like a mad thing, but it's terrible at going round corners. In other words it's utterly useless unless you fancy towing the world's fastest caravan.

Power: *500bhp*

0-60mph: *3.8 seconds*

Top Speed: *190mph*

Price: *£70,000*

Cool rating: 😎😎

Dodge Viper
SRT-10

34

Bentley

Flying Spur

BENTLEY

Going fast isn't just a young man's game. Even slightly podgy old men with no hair like to go fast, but preferably if someone else is doing the driving. Which must be why the Bentley Flying Spur exists.

This stealth 600bhp 6.0-litre 12-cylinder limousine weighs almost 2.5 tonnes and is more spacious and luxurious inside than most five-star hotel rooms. But it can still hit 200mph and find 60mph in 4.5 seconds. Which is utterly bonkers when you think about it.

It's not great at going round corners though, so it's probably best to simply clamber into the back, put your slippers on, your feet up and let Jeeves do all the hard work.

 Power: 600bhp

 0-60mph: 4.5 seconds

 Top Speed: 200mph

 Price: £140,000

 Cool rating:

Subaru made its name winning every rally going and then bunging all the technology from that into its road cars. Because of this, the Impreza is regarded as the only choice if you have to tackle a lot of winding country roads and are in an awful hurry. (Maybe if you're a burglar who's just robbed a chicken farm.)

Lots of whooshy turbo power, bags of four-wheel drive grip, ridiculous-looking wings, spoilers everywhere and incredibly ugly styling all add up to one of the greatest yet most embarrassing cars in this book.

We love it, but wouldn't want anyone to see us driving it.

 Power: 296bhp

 0-60mph: 4.8 seconds

 Top Speed: 155mph

 Price: £26,000

 Cool rating:

35

Subaru Impreza
WRX STi

If you're going to name a car after the man that started the company, it had better be seriously good. And the boffins at Ferrari made sure the Enzo was the best.

Back in 2003 when it went on sale, the Enzo was ridiculously high-tech, with a skeleton chassis made entirely of carbon fibre and a 6.0-litre V12 that borrowed ideas from Ferrari's championship-winning Formula 1 cars.

There is a drawback to making cars this fast though. Only 400 Enzos ever left the Ferrari factory, and after a series of very high-profile accidents, there are a fair few less than that still on the road today.

 Power: 650bhp

 0-60mph: 3.14 seconds

 Top Speed: 218mph

 Price: £450,000

 Cool rating:

'...er F...Ferrari it's hard to think of anything that can match it.'

36

Ferrari
Enzo

MO 140 EF

ferrari

A few years ago, Porsche promised building a brand new racing car, but for reasons known only to German men, mid-way results, they suddenly decided to stop building this super racer. A lot of money spent already. Porsche decided to switch from the idea into a road car... And so it became a road car. All the right materials, the way to make the lovely Porsche so good... This idea would have been proven too good to throw away. All the components used for...

The world's greatest supercars had, until the 1990s, tended to come from Italy. But now the world's greatest supercars tend to rule, and at the top of the pile, many Carrera GT which makes most other cars look silly.

Power	612 bhp
0-60mph	3.9 seconds
Top Speed	205mph
Price	£330,000
Cool rating	

Carrera GT

S·GO 612

'The most **exciting** road-going car Porsche has ever made.'

Porsche Carrera GT

37

Where the BMW M3 and Audi RS4 have to make do with measly 4 and 4.2-litre V8s to get around, the Mercedes C63 AMG gets one with 6.2 litres. That's a lot more, and more, as we all know, is better.

This means it has more power than its rivals of course, but more importantly, much more torque. Torque is weird and we don't really understand it, but it's what you'd use to pull a tree out of the ground. Or to accelerate like a nuclear missile when you needed to overtake something slow and annoying.

The C63 AMG is essentially just that, a nuclear missile with wheels. Be careful where you point it!

 Power: *457bhp*

 0-60mph: *5.2 seconds*

 Top Speed: *155mph*

 Price: *£50,000*

 Cool rating:

Mercedes C63
AMG

38

It doesn't always take a big engine and an even bigger price tag to make a great car. In fact, Renault keep coming up with some of the best sports cars in the world with only cheap little hatchbacks to choose from.

The secret is to make them lighter, so they're faster, and then make them handle like go-karts. The Megane R26R only gets 227bhp from its tiny 2.0-litre engine, but it's so light and agile that it can keep up with things that have twice the power.

The real beauty of making cars light and simple doesn't make them more expensive. So the R26R is the same price as your average, and very boring, Ford Mondeo.

 Power: 227bhp

 0-60mph: 6.0 seconds

 Top Speed: 147mph

 Price: £23,000

 Cool rating:

39

Renault Megane
R26R

'The fastest front-wheel drive car round the Nürburgring.'

40

Maserati

MC12

How does Maserati go about building a car to beat the Ferrari Enzo? Simple. It buys a Ferrari Enzo, paints it white and sticks Maserati badges on it. Then sells it to people like Jay Kay, who've already got an Enzo.

Now Ferrari actually owned Maserati at the time when the MC12 and Enzo were being made, so really this was just a cunning way of making people buy the same car twice. And considering either cost well over £400,000, you'd want to know that the MC12 was worth it. But as it happens it probably wasn't. For starters it was slower, and to make matters worse you couldn't get over speed bumps or see out of the back.

 Power: *620bhp*

 0-60mph: *3.8 seconds*

 Top Speed: *205mph*

 Price: *£520,000*

 Cool rating:

40

Ariel Atom
Supercharged

41

In the old days it was essential when designing a proper Italian supercar to make it extremely noisy, uncomfortable, almost impossible to get into, or out of, and then paint it a sickening colour.

But at some point about ten years ago everybody realised this wasn't the best way of selling lots of cars. Everyone, that is, except Lamborghini.

The LP670 is a brash, expensive and almost completely pointless car which, for all of those reasons and more besides, we absolutely love. It is huge for starters, yet tiny inside, and its 661bhp V12 makes the sort of racket that gives horses heart attacks. It also has scissor doors, and those you can't live without. Or live with, come to that.

Power: *661bhp*

0-60mph: *3.2 seconds*

Top Speed: *212mph*

Price: *£266,000*

Cool rating:

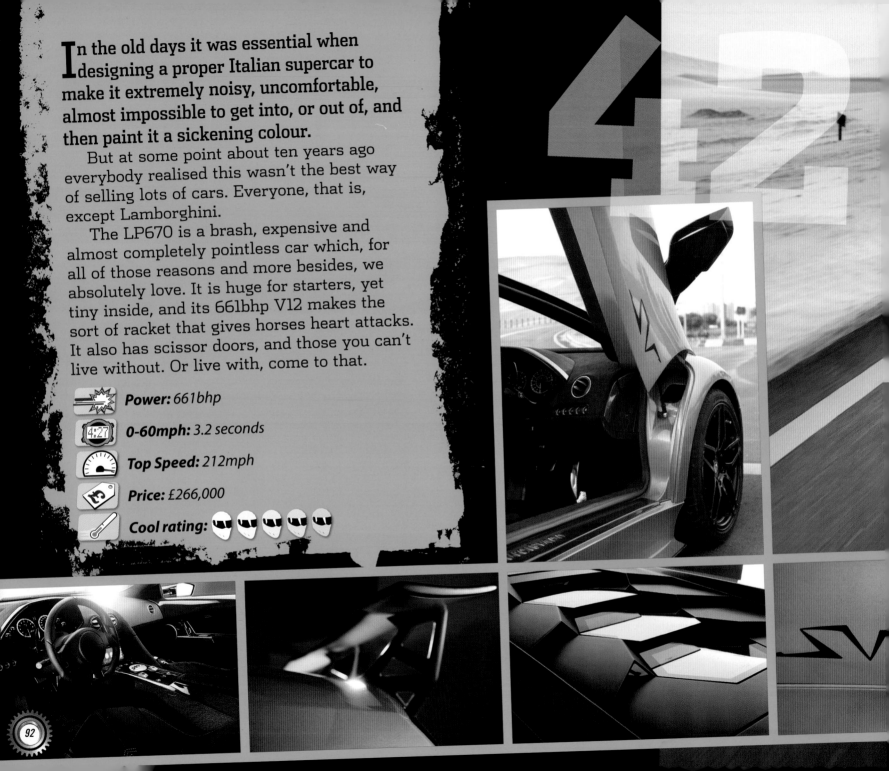

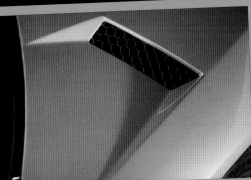

Lamborghini
LP670-4SV

42

'The fastest
Lamborghini
ever made.'

43

The Ford GT was so wide, so thirsty, so fast and so flash that one of the first people in the world to buy it was a certain Jeremy Clarkson. Who would have guessed?

But there were a few hitches along the way. It took absolutely ages to arrive. And the price kept creeping up while he waited. And when it finally did get to Casa Del Clarkson the alarm kept going off in the middle of the night. It also drank so much fuel that it couldn't get him to work in the mornings on a single tank.

But it did have a 5.3-litre twin supercharged V8 that could hit 100mph in 7.4 seconds and keep going until the needle said 205. So Jeremy was happy.

Power: 550bhp

0-60mph: 3.5 seconds

Top Speed: 205mph

Price: £121,000

Cool rating:

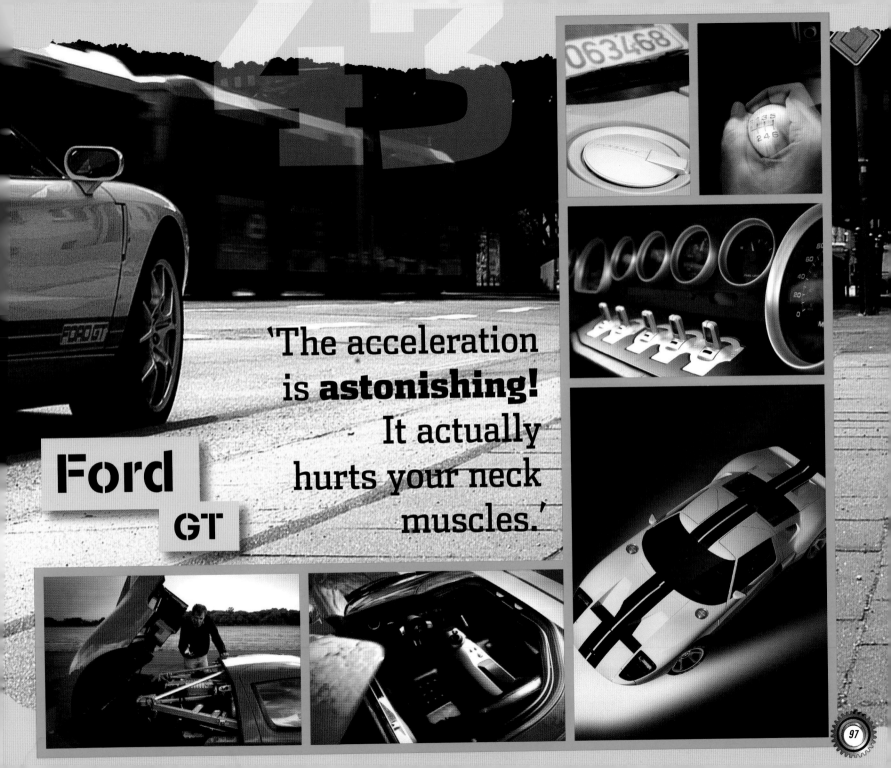

'The acceleration is **astonishing!** It actually hurts your neck muscles.'

Ford GT

Hang on a minute. How did this get in here? Oh well, technically it's last once the Stig has dished out a few lessons.

The Chevrolet Lacetti has been the (only) choice for our Star in a Reasonably Priced Car for years now and it's still going strong. The fastest one they sell only has 119bhp, takes ten seconds to get to 60mph and is lucky if it ever gets over 100mph, but we've learnt to love it.

And remember that you can get your hands on one for just over £13,000, which is a bargain for the car that has lapped the *Top Gear* track more than any other.

Power: 119bhp

0-60mph: 9.8 seconds

Top Speed: 121mph

Price: £13,500

Cool rating: 0

Chevrolet Lacetti

44

99

The Vanquish is a car we all love, even if we know it's a tiny bit rubbish. Built a few years ago to take on the might of Ferrari, it's actually full of parts from the old Ford Mondeo, so it didn't stand much of a chance.

To make matters worse, it had one of the first and most hopeless flappy-paddle gearboxes. This exploded at least four or five times a day, leaving premiership footballers crying on the hard shoulder all over the country.

None of this mattered a jot though, because the Vanquish didn't really need to go anywhere. Even today we reckon this is one of the best-looking supercars ever.

Power: *520bhp*

0-60mph: *4.8 seconds*

Top Speed: *200mph*

Price: *£177,000*

Cool rating:

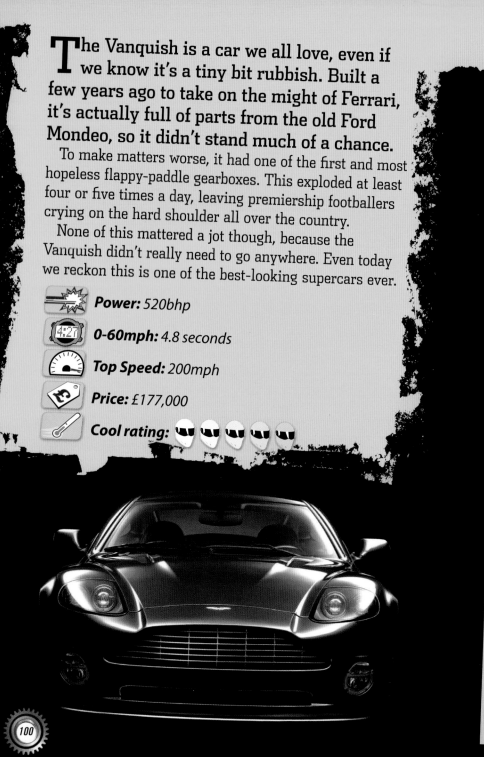

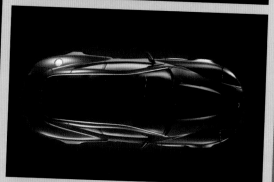

45

Aston Martin
Vanquish S

Honda Civic
Type-R

46

RX56 TZD

102

Hot hatches usually look pretty dull. Essentially just really dull cars, but with slightly bigger wheels and jazzy paint. Now the Honda Civic Type-R had a head start in this department, because the normal Civic already looked like it had come from another planet.

Give it the Type-R treatment and it still looks like it came from another planet, but at warp speed.

It gets the outer space theme on the inside too, with millions of luminous dials and switches, most of which you're too afraid to touch.

It's not actually as fast as those bonkers looks suggest, which means Jeremy absolutely hates it, but real world speed doesn't matter when you're doing warp speed in your head.

 Power: *198bhp*

 0-60mph: *7.4 seconds*

 Top Speed: *140mph*

 Price: *£19,000*

 Cool rating:

Jeremy hates to admit that going fast isn't always about power, but the fifth fastest car round the *Top Gear* track definitely proves the point. The Caterham Superlight R500 has about as much oomph as your average hot hatch, but it only weighs 506kg. This adds up to 0-60mph in 2.88 seconds and a top speed of 150mph, and that's a lot in a car without a roof or doors, especially when the windscreen is an optional extra.

The most powerful car in the world, the Bugatti Veyron, took almost half a second longer to get round our track than the Caterham, and you can only buy one of them for the same price as twenty-five R500s. Which would be useless, but that's still a lot of cars.

 Power: *263bhp*

 0-60mph: *2.8 seconds*

 Top Speed: *150mph*

 Price: *£42,200*

 Cool rating:

'It moves with the agility of a **flea.**'

Caterham
Superlight R500

The Scuderia is the Ferrari F430's leaner, meaner, younger brother. Put on a strict diet, made even more powerful and with a bucketload of computer wizardry thrown in, the Scud brought Formula 1 technology to the high street when it appeared in 2007.

Handling it was no easy feat. Enzo would have had tracks, but far easier for your average Joe to drive. And, at less than half the price, it was also more affordable. Well, sort of... €170,000 is still quite a lot of money.

All Scuderias also come with racing stripes running the whole length of the car, which we have to pretend to disapprove of, but secretly want to stroke when no one's looking.

Power 510bhp

0-60mph 3.6 seconds

Top Speed 198mph

Price €170,000

Cool rating

'Listen to that noise... you just have to **flex** your big toe!'

Ferrari F430
Scuderia

SCUDERIA

48

48

The Golf GTI is widely regarded as the best all-rounder in the world. Meaning it's just as happy taking your mum to the shops as it is the Stig round our track. But now VW has thrown a spanner in the works by unveiling something it's calling the Golf R.

This is a much more powerful version of the GTI, but this time it also has four-wheel drive, which means better grip in the corners too. Which means you can go faster. Which means we now want a Volkswagen more than we want a Ford Focus RS. Oh dear. That wasn't meant to happen.

 Power: *267bhp*

 0-60mph: *5.7 seconds*

 Top Speed: *155mph*

 Price: *£30,000*

 Cool rating:

49

VW Golf
R

There is a fly in the ointment at Ferrari. Having just launched the truly breathtaking 458 Italia, they have learned that back in Britain, where it is rainy and mostly just full of Vauxhalls, a car is about to emerge that may boot their new baby off pole position.

The McLaren MP4-12C is a mouthful to say, but it's one you should probably practise. Here is the successor to the McLaren F1, a supercar still regarded by most people as the greatest ever, despite being twenty years old.

The MP4-12C will use technology from McLaren's Formula 1 racing cars and the latest ideas from scientific boffins to be incredibly fast but also economical and nice to the environment. Look out Ferrari, the British are coming...

 Power: *600bhp*

 0-60mph: *3.0 seconds (approx)*

 Top Speed: *200+mph*

 Price: *£160,000 (approx)*

 Cool rating:

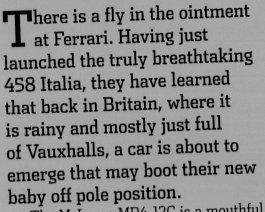

50

McLaren
MP4-12C